T0065749

ECCLESIASTES

A TIME FOR EVERYTHING

7 Studies for Individuals or Groups

STEPHEN BOARD

SHAW

WATERBROOK
PRESS

Ecclesiastes
A SHAW BOOK
PUBLISHED BY WATERBROOK PRESS
2375 Telstar Drive, Suite 160
Colorado Springs, CO 80920
A division of Random House, Inc.

Unless otherwise indicated, all Scripture quotations are taken from the
Holy Bible: New International Version ® *NIV* ® Copyright © 1973, 1978,
1984 by International Bible Society. Used by permission of Zondervan
Publishing House. All rights reserved.

ISBN: 978-0-87788-206-0

Cover photo by Stephen Board

Printed in the United States of America

146502721

CONTENTS

INTRODUCTION

"All is vanity!" "A time for everything." "There's nothing new under the sun." Ecclesiastes is one of those books of the Bible that everyone quotes, but not too many people actually study. Yet few portions of the Bible carry the wallop of Ecclesiastes. Thomas Wolfe pronounced, "Of all that I have ever seen or learned, [Ecclesiastes] seems to me the noblest, the wisest, and the most powerful expression of man's life upon this earth." The questions raised in this book immediately resonate with the typical modern person, who is often suspended between a vaguely religious background and a schedule packed with this-worldly tasks and toys. Like the rest of the Bible, Ecclesiastes assumes that almost everyone retains some mental concept of God. It's just that this mental concept doesn't figure much into their day-to-day decisions.

If ordinary human life were always 100 percent joyful or always 100 percent dreadful, it would raise no hard questions and present us with no forks in the road. The facts are, as Ecclesiastes teaches, that most people find their lives a mix of happiness and unhappiness—with no control over the mix. Time and chance happen to all. Hovering over the richest, most fulfilled life is the brutal fact of death.

"So what's it all for?" the author asks. "Is everything meaningless?" Ecclesiastes picks away at these questions of life, sorting through the kinds of solutions most people turn to for meaning—career, money, pleasure, wisdom, shrewd business dealings, a good family life. But life "under the sun" only gets so good. Aldous Huxley echoed this theme when he said, "There comes a time when one asks even of Shakespeare, even of Beethoven, 'Is this all?'" After reading Ecclesiastes, no one can dismiss the Bible as being unrealistic.

Yet here and there, like moonlight diffused through clouds, the book hints that there is indeed more to being human than most people think. Life may run short of meaning and ultimately run out, but in the end, it is God, the maker of all things (11:5), who anchors all human joy and pain (2:24). He holds our meaning in his grasp and becomes thereby the "whole point" or "duty" of everyone (12:13).

As I studied this book, I was reminded of how the Bible's message is not for everyone. It's not for the self-righteous or for people who don't need anybody but themselves. It's not for people who are completely satisfied with their lives and assume things will always be that way. But for realists and those who know they are sinners, its message can explain and transform life. May you find this to be true as you study this timeless book.

HOW TO USE THIS STUDYGUIDE

Fisherman studyguides are based on the inductive approach to Bible study. Inductive study is discovery study; we discover what the Bible says as we ask questions about its content and search for answers. This is quite different from the process in which a teacher *tells* a group *about* the Bible, what it means, and what to do about it. In inductive study, God speaks directly to each of us through his Word.

A group functions best when a leader keeps the discussion on target, but this leader is neither the teacher nor the "answer person." A leader's responsibility is to *ask*—not *tell*. The answers come from the text itself as group members examine, discuss, and think together about the passage.

There are four kinds of questions in each study. The first is an *approach question*. Used before the Bible passage is read, this question breaks the ice and helps you focus on the topic of the Bible study. It begins to reveal where thoughts and feelings need to be transformed by Scripture.

Some of the earlier questions in each study are *observation questions* designed to help you find out basic facts—who, what, where, when, and how.

When you know what the Bible says, you need to ask, *What does it mean?* These *interpretation questions* help you to discover the writer's basic message.

Application questions ask *What does it mean to me?* They challenge you to live out the Scripture's life-transforming message.

Fisherman studyguides provide spaces between questions for jotting down responses and related questions you would like to raise in the group. Each group member should have a copy of the studyguide and may take a turn in leading the group.

For consistency, Fisherman guides are written from the *New International Version.* But a group should feel free to use the NIV or any other accurate, modern translation of the Bible such as the *New Living Translation,* the *New Revised Standard Version,* the *New Jerusalem Bible,* or the *Good News Bible.* (Other paraphrases of the Bible may be referred to when additional help is needed.) Bible commentaries should not be brought to a Bible study because they tend to dampen discussion and keep people from thinking for themselves.

SUGGESTIONS FOR GROUP LEADERS

1. Read and study the Bible passage thoroughly beforehand, grasping its themes and applying its teachings for yourself. Pray that the Holy Spirit will "guide you into truth" so that your leadership will guide others.

2. If the studyguide's questions ever seem ambiguous or unnatural to you, rephrase them, feeling free to add others that seem necessary to bring out the meaning of a verse.

3. Begin (and end) the study promptly. Start by asking someone to pray for God's help. Remember, the Holy Spirit is the teacher, not you!

4. Ask for volunteers to read the passages out loud.

5. As you ask the studyguide's questions in sequence, encourage everyone to participate in the discussion. If some are silent, ask,

"What do you think, Heather?" or "Dan, what can you add to that answer?" or suggest, "Let's have an answer from someone who hasn't spoken up yet."

6. If a question comes up that you can't answer, don't be afraid to admit that you're baffled! Assign the topic as a research project for someone to report on next week.

7. Keep the discussion moving and focused. Though tangents will inevitably be introduced, you can bring the discussion back to the topic at hand. Learn to pace the discussion so that you finish a study each session you meet.

8. Don't be afraid of silences; some questions take time to answer and some people need time to gather courage to speak. If silence persists, rephrase your question, but resist the temptation to answer it yourself.

9. If someone comes up with an answer that is clearly illogical or unbiblical, ask him or her for further clarification: "What verse suggests that to you?"

10. Discourage Bible-hopping and overuse of cross-references. Learn all you can from *this* passage, along with a few important references suggested in the studyguide.

11. Some questions are marked with a ♦. This indicates that further information is available in the Leader's Notes at the back of the guide.

12. For further information on getting a new Bible study group started and keeping it functioning effectively, read Gladys Hunt's *You Can Start a Bible Study Group* and *Pilgrims in Progress: Growing through Groups* by Jim and Carol Plueddemann.

SUGGESTIONS FOR GROUP MEMBERS

1. Learn and apply the following ground rules for effective Bible study. (If new members join the group later, review these guidelines with the whole group.)

2. Remember that your goal is to learn all that you can *from the Bible passage being studied.* Let it speak for itself without using Bible commentaries or other Bible passages. There is more than enough in each assigned passage to keep your group productively occupied for one session. Sticking to the passage saves the group from insecurity and confusion.

3. Avoid the temptation to bring up those fascinating tangents that don't really grow out of the passage you are discussing. If the topic is of common interest, you can bring it up later in informal conversation following the study. Meanwhile, help each other stick to the subject!

4. Encourage each other to participate. People remember best what they discover and verbalize for themselves. Some people are naturally shier than others, or they may be afraid of making a mistake. If your discussion is free and friendly and you show real interest in what other group members think and feel, they will be more likely to speak up. Remember, the more people involved in a discussion, the richer it will be.

5. Guard yourself from answering too many questions or talking too much. Give others a chance to express themselves. If you are one who participates easily, discipline yourself by counting to ten before you open your mouth!

6. Make personal, honest applications and commit yourself to letting God's Word change you.

LIFE UNDER THE SUN

Ecclesiastes 1–2

The first two chapters of Ecclesiastes help us get acquainted with the themes and tone of voice of an author who simply refers to himself as "the Teacher." This ancient writing is one of the poetic books of the Bible, along with Psalms, Job, and Proverbs. As poetry, the language may at times seem to overstate its case or present one way of looking at reality which may seem new to you. However, you will soon discover that the Teacher's questions are really ones we all ask.

The main theme is human happiness. What does it take to make us happy? What is worth our energy and time in the quest for happiness? And is this life "under the sun" able to deliver on our expectation that we ought to be happy? These are some of the Teacher's underlying questions and doubts. Is the author finally a pessimist about life? See what you decide as you study this book.

1. In his novel *Moby Dick,* Herman Melville observed, "That mortal man who hath more of joy than sorrow in him, that mortal man cannot be true—not true, or

undeveloped. The truest of all men was the Man of Sorrows, and the truest of all books is . . . Ecclesiastes."
Do you agree that there's something "untrue" or wrong about people who seem too happy? Why or why not?

Read Ecclesiastes 1:1-15.

◆ **2.** Who is the author and what do you learn about him?

◆ **3.** Name the realities that cause the author's unhappiness with the world as he finds it "under the sun."

4. According to this passage, what in the natural order is under our control and what is beyond our control?

13

Read Ecclesiastes 1:16–2:16.

5. What actions does the king take in response to the apparent indifference of the world? Look for all the verbs of action and decision.

6. A lifestyle refers to one's values expressed in a pattern of choices: what we spend money on, how we devote our time, what obsesses us. How many different lifestyles does the author adopt here in his quest?

What are some modern parallels?

♦ **7.** In each of these pursuits, what is under one's control, if anything, and what is beyond one's control?

8. How is wisdom better than folly (1:18; 2:13-16)?
How is it not better than folly?

Read Ecclesiastes 2:17-26.

9. Why does he hate life at this point (verses 17-23)?

Is this disappointment with the world a view that only an older person could hold, or might it also be a view of youth? Explain.

◆ **10.** Even if the biblical author has come to hate life, he is not an ascetic and not world-denying. What are the points of satisfaction he commends in verses 17-26?

What new fact about life conditions all our happiness?

11. From 2:24-26 we can learn a number of useful facts about God. Can you identify three?

12. How do the final verses of chapter 2 point a way out of complete despair about our own happiness?

13. What observations in these first two chapters of Ecclesiastes ring true to your experience?

What hope can you gain from the Teacher's searching?

A MIX OF TIME AND CHANCE

Ecclesiastes 3–4

In the first two chapters, Solomon reflected on the normal experience of life as a flow of events beyond our control, with an inevitable and predictable end in death. He also introduced the "God fact," that is, our happiness can still survive in this world but as a gift of God's pleasure to us (2:24-25). Someone has said that a big problem with being an atheist is that, when you feel really grateful about something in your life, you have no one to thank. Ecclesiastes reminds us who to thank in good and bad times.

Before he became a Christian, Charles Colson had the following spiritual experience. Taking his ten-year-old son boating, he watched "the joy of discovery in his eyes, the thrill of feeling the wind's power in his hands. I found myself in that one unforgettable moment quietly talking to God. . . . 'Thank you, God, for giving me this son, for giving us this wonderful moment. Just looking now into this boy's eyes fulfills my life. Whatever happens in the future, even if I die tomorrow, my life is complete and full. Thank you.'"

1. Have you ever had an unexpected experience that made you well up with joy and thanksgiving? Describe it.

Read Ecclesiastes 3:1-15.

♦ **2.** What do you think is the point of the list of rhythms or opposites described in verses 1-8?

3. "Fatalism" is a world view that there is no way to avoid what happens. Does the material in this section support fatalism? Why or why not?

♦ **4.** Though we are creatures of time, we also have eternity implanted within our hearts (verse 11). What evidences of this truth have you seen in your experience or in the lives of others?

5. Changing his pessimistic tone to a positive one, what does the Teacher affirm (verses 11-14)?

Read Ecclesiastes 3:16–4:3.

♦ **6.** Our material frailty can make us feel like mere animals. In what ways are human beings similar to animals according to the Teacher (3:18-21)? In what ways are we different (compare also with 3:11)?

7. Solomon will not let us forget the severe limitations of happiness on earth: we are creatures of time and victims of what looks like chance. What *new* negative realities are faced in this passage?

8. Since there is a God, Ecclesiastes says, he does deal with human wickedness. God also intrudes on our thinking, feeling, and living. Which verses speak of God's involvement in human life?

Read Ecclesiastes 4:4-16.

9. What different styles of and motivations for work are described in verses 4-9?

Do you see similar styles and motivations in our day? Explain.

10. People's evil actions are part of the problem in human society (as we see in the first few verses of chapter 4). Now the Teacher implies that people may be part of the solution as well (verses 8-12). How might this work out in daily life?

♦ **11.** Christian doctrine is always based on the whole teaching of the Bible. However, see if you can try to construct a brief "doctrine of God"—truths about who God is—based on Ecclesiastes 2:24–4:16.

Likewise, can you construct a "doctrine of man"?
What might you wish for more revelation about from
other passages of Scripture?

12. Once again, notice here what is in our control and
what is not. Is there a course of action laid out in
these two chapters we can take when we feel panic
that life is out of our control?

MAKING THE MOST OF IT

Ecclesiastes 5–6

At some point in early adulthood, most of us come to terms with life as it is rather than as we wished it would be. We decide to play the hand we're dealt, to use one analogy. The talents, good looks, wealth, opportunities, or lack of these, up to that point in our lives then become the raw material for whatever we will make of ourselves. The older generation calls this "maturity." Not everyone agrees: "The reasonable man adapts himself to the world: the unreasonable one persists in trying to adapt the world to himself. Therefore all progress depends on the unreasonable man" (George Bernard Shaw). Here the Teacher gives us warnings and wisdom for making our way in this life.

♦ **1.** When is resisting the way the world works noble and right, and when is it foolish? Can you give an example?

Read Ecclesiastes 5:1-7.

2. What can we learn about God in these verses? about ourselves?

3. Why should God care about our vows?

Read Ecclesiastes 5:8-20.

4. Identify the various economic strata or levels mentioned in these verses.

5. What are the pluses and minuses of life as poor, rich, powerful, or weak?

6. What components of the "good life" are mentioned here (verses 18-20)?

How does God figure into it?

7. Does the "good life" in our time differ from the good life in Solomon's time? How?

♦ **8.** Reflecting on one's life is a big part of the message of Ecclesiastes. Yet verse 20 seems to suggest that some people don't reflect and don't need to. How do you explain that?

Read Ecclesiastes 6.

9. What are the assets and liabilities of the individual in this chapter (verses 1-6)?

Assets   Liabilities

10. Note the questions asked in this chapter. What is their purpose? How do you answer them?

11. Ecclesiastes 6 seems to imply that we have so much uncertainty in life that we can't arrive at the "good life." What argument would you use to counter that sentiment?

12. Socrates said the unexamined life is not worth living. What are the major obstacles for modern people to examine their lives and achieve a life worth living?

WISDOM IS WORTH THE TROUBLE

Ecclesiastes 7–8

Put a moth on an oriental rug, and we can excuse it for thinking the world is all red or gold—or whatever is in its vision. Only from a distance is the intricate pattern obvious, and then only from a viewpoint outside the rug. The moth knows the truth but not the "whole truth." Ecclesiastes sometimes takes the viewpoint of the moth and sometimes that of the outside observer. It would agree with twentieth century philosopher Ludwig Wittgenstein who said, "The sense of the world must remain outside of the world."

The Teacher reminds us of our ignorance about life. We can be sure of some things, puzzled or even angry about others, but we can never really make sense of it all on our own. We are moths trying to see a pattern. But part of wisdom is not letting this fact bother us. We have our hands full relating to what we do understand, and the wise person can find joy and gladness once he leaves the mysteries to a sovereign Creator God.

28

1. Relate a time when there was a big difference between the way you looked at a situation or event and the way your children or your parents looked at it. Did you have different facts or just a different perspective?

◆ **Read Ecclesiastes 7:1-12.**

◆ **2.** Becoming wise is a process. What things does the author suggest will help a person become wise?

3. What things may hinder or defeat a person in becoming wise?

Read Ecclesiastes 7:13–8:1.

4. We can learn something from our own reactions to things in life. The Teacher assumes we will be puzzled by what two common bewildering experiences (7:13-14)?

How do you respond to these conclusions? Why?

5. Being realistic about life is a big theme in Ecclesiastes. Verses 15-25 point out some ways we can
deceive ourselves or let others deceive us. Look for
three or more.

6. The world is a dangerous place in relationships.
What has Solomon found out about both men and
women?

7. In the end, how is wisdom a positive thing (7:11-12,
19; 8:1)?

Read Ecclesiastes 8:2-17.

8. Paying heed to the inevitabilities of life is another major theme in Ecclesiastes. Look for what is inevitable in these verses.

♦ **9.** What makes joy possible in light of the picture presented in verses 14-17?

10. Both Ecclesiastes 7 and 8 suggest a sovereign God in the background of all we see "under the sun." Looking back over these two chapters, what references to God do you find that suggest his past, present, or future authority?

11. Can you be content with not understanding everything? What parts of your life are you most uncomfortable not understanding? Has anything in this chapter helped with that?

MORE PRACTICAL WISDOM UNDER THE SUN

Ecclesiastes 9:1–11:6

The "collector of proverbs" continues to give us short-term strategies for a realistic life. Such a life takes into account the big picture: the inevitability of death, the possibility of tragedy and injustice, and the rays of sunlight that still shine out from the cracks in a fallen world, because a sovereign God—the ultimate environment—"favors what you do" (9:7).

Again, the opening verses argue that the fact of our eventual demise conditions our behavior. Speaking to this reality, Blaise Pascal observed: "We must live differently in the world according to these different assumptions: (1) that we could always remain in it; (2) that it is certain that we shall not remain here long, and uncertain if we shall remain here one hour. This last assumption is our condition."

♦ **1.** What are some ways modern people cope with the prospect of their own eventual demise?

Read Ecclesiastes 9.

2. From this passage, how does Ecclesiastes deal with the finiteness and shortness of life? (Compare this with your answers to question 1.)

3. This chapter cites several disappointments in life and several real joys. List as many as you see.

4. What "edge" does wisdom give a person in dealing with life's uncertainties?

5. With what hope are we left (verses 1, 7)?

33

Read Ecclesiastes 10.

6. How many examples can you find in this chapter
where the situation seems backward from how it ought
to be?

7. Even with these realities, the author does not seem
to despair. How do you avoid cynicism and despair
when things seem to work out backward and hopelessly?

8. What are the marks of and hazards that accompany
a lifestyle of "folly" (verses 1-18)?

Read Ecclesiastes 11:1-6.

◆ **9.** Earlier, the writer argued that "time and chance"
happen to all (9:11). With these proverbial counsels he
suggests that you can "beat the odds." Does this seem
contradictory to you, or just a qualification of the
underlying reality? Explain.

10. Verses 1-6 encourage the taking of risks. Why should we take risks?

♦ **11.** The author of Ecclesiastes pushes us to think hard about what we are living for and what should truly bother us in the world under the sun. Yet, not everyone gets around to that. Why do so many people not give their lives a thought?

♦ **12.** Review these chapters. Where is God in all the time and chance of life?

How does a knowledge of God help you in your daily life?

THE END OF THE MATTER

Ecclesiastes 11:7–12:14

The Teacher winds down his reflections on life by evaluating the beginning and ending years. A recent survey determined that most people think the middle years of life are their happiest. And most people don't want to repeat any earlier period, such as their teen years, even if it would mean restoring some of their youth. Ecclesiastes closes with a word of wisdom for youth and a description of the latter years of life.

1. If you could, would you want to repeat any younger period of your life? Why or why not?

36

Read Ecclesiastes 11:7–12:8.

♦ **2.** What are the characteristic marks of youth that Ecclesiastes acknowledges (11:9-10)?

3. How does the reality of God affect the lifestyle of the wise young person in these verses?

4. Why is the advice given in 12:1 important?

♦ **5.** Review the whole book's understanding of God as Creator in these earlier references.

3:11:

5:19:

7:29:

11:5:

6. If we remember God in our youth, what are the benefits?

7. Why do young people sometimes think their happiness is diminished by attention to God in their youthful years?

◆ **8.** The aging experience is rightly understood to be a process of subtraction, moving toward the final subtraction of earthly life itself. These verses use vivid imagery to describe various realities of the latter years of life. Which can you readily identify?

◆ **9.** What counsel, if any, does Ecclesiastes give us for coping with these diminutions of earthly pleasure?

Read Ecclesiastes 12:9-14.

◆ **10.** What does the author reveal or disclose about the source and character of his wisdom (verses 9-12)?

11. What is assumed or taught in the "conclusion of the matter" (verses 13-14) about the following:

human beings:

God:

God's revelation:

the present:

the future:

◆ **12.** Solomon's conclusion: In the end, we are commended the fear of God and a lifestyle of obeying his commandments. Is this enough to cope with the many grim realities of earthly life, old age, death, and the vanity of it all? What more would you like to know?

13. Thinking back over this study, which of the themes in Ecclesiastes are most instructive for you? Which are most troubling? Why?

14. If you had nothing else of the Bible but the book of Ecclesiastes, would you feel you could still understand and rejoice in your life under the sun and under God?

STUDY 7

ECCLESIASTES AND THE WHOLE BIBLE

Selected Passages

One writer calls Ecclesiastes the Bible's "night before Christmas." The darkness of human life expressed by the Teacher anticipated a day when a light would come and shine in the darkness, "the true light that gives light to every man" (John 1:9). Many themes from Ecclesiastes are echoed throughout the Old and New Testaments. This study will look at some of these themes in other parts of Scripture to compare how they expand on or fulfill the Teacher's observations. Seen in the light of the whole of Scripture, we find that the message of Ecclesiastes is true and ultimately hopeful.

1. What question or theme from your study of Ecclesiastes sticks with you the most? Why?

42

◆ **2.** Read the following passages and discuss the ideas that echo or expand on the themes of Ecclesiastes we have studied.

Psalm 49:5-15:

1 Timothy 6:6-10:

1 Timothy 6:17-19:

James 4:13-17:

1 Peter 3:8-17:

◆ **3.** The New Testament uses the term "meaningless" or "vanity" in the same way Ecclesiastes uses it—to indicate emptiness, frustration, and poverty of meaning. Read the passage below in two Bible translations. What does this passage suggest is the source of human world-weariness?

> For the creature was made subject to vanity, not willingly, but by reason of him who hath subjected the same in hope, because the creature itself also shall be delivered from the bondage of corruption into the glorious liberty of the children of God. (Romans 8:20-21, KJV).

> For the creation was subjected to frustration, not by its own choice, but by the will of the one who subjected it, in hope that the creation itself will be liberated from its

bondage to decay and brought into the glorious freedom of the children of God. (Romans 8:20-21, NIV).

4. This Romans 8 passage above implies the created order suffers a deep lack imposed by God. How does that fact compare to what the Teacher observes in Ecclesiastes 1:13 and 3:10?

5. Remembering "what a heavy burden God has laid on men," what hope or resolution of the vanity the creation lives under does Romans 8:20-21 give?

6. Overall, has your life echoed more the pessimism of Ecclesiastes or the positive tones of the entire biblical message? Why?

♦ **7.** Ecclesiastes may well be the Bible's "night before Christmas," meaning it shows the limits of human life without the New Testament fulfillment in Christ. What aspects of your Christian life and faith give you a basis for rising above world weariness, pessimism, and vanity?

LEADER'S NOTES

■ **Study 1/Life Under the Sun**

Question 2. The name "Teacher" (or "Preacher" in some versions) comes from the Hebrew word *Koheleth,* meaning "leader of the assembly" in the temple or synagogue. The Greek word for "assembly" is *ecclesia,* from which comes the name of the book of Ecclesiastes.

Traditional Jewish and Christian thought has been that King Solomon is the author (based on Ecclesiastes 1:1, 12-17). The book itself does not explicitly claim to be Solomon's work, unlike Proverbs and the Song of Songs. Some modern scholars would say it was a poetic voice in "Solomonic" tones. The concluding portion in Ecclesiastes 12 appears to be written in a different voice than the rest of the book, whether by artistic design or historical sequence. For this study, we will refer to the author as Solomon and understand these qualifications on the name.

For further study, two excellent commentaries are Derek Kidner's *A Time to Mourn and a Time to Dance* (Downers Grove, IL: InterVarsity Press, 1976), now issued in *The Message of Ecclesiastes* (Downers Grove, IL: InterVarsity Press, 1985); and Michael Eaton's *Ecclesiastes* in the Tyndale Old Testament Series (Downers Grove, IL: InterVarsity Press, 1983).

Question 3. The theme of meaninglessness, or its alternate translations of "utter vanity, futile, pointless, emptiness" (New English Bible), derives meaning from its usage in context throughout Ecclesiastes. As you work through the chapters, formulate your own synonyms based on its context.

Also, help your group notice in the first two chapters what is permanent and what is temporary. What is remembered and what is forgotten? What is under one's control and what is out of one's control? These are issues that dominate the rest of the book and will be useful questions every session.

Question 7. On this quest for happiness from acquiring, consider discussing G. K. Chesterton's solution: "There are two ways to get enough: one is to accumulate more and more. The other is to desire less."

Question 10. The author has already mentioned that this life under the sun is a "heavy burden" God has given us (Ecclesiastes 1:13). These closing verses help us see that Ecclesiastes does not deny the world-weary conclusions of this passage. They are true, but they are not the *whole* truth.

■ Study 2/A Mix of Time and Chance

Questions 2 and 3. Fatalism would be one way to take the list of rhythms in Ecclesiastes 3:1-8, but one might better take the list as a description of the variety and diversity of life's experiences.

Question 4. It is important to see how the dilemmas and message of Ecclesiastes are relevant to our lives today, and that many people wrestle with these enduring questions. As you go through each study, it may be helpful to read the various suggested modern quotes featured in these notes and discuss how they echo the themes in Ecclesiastes.

In what ways does this quote by Blaise Pascal (1623-1662) reflect or expand on the Teacher's thoughts in this passage?

When I consider the brief span of my life absorbed into the eternity which comes before and after—as the memory of a guest who tarries but a day—the small space I occupy and which I see swallowed up in the infinite immensity of spaces of which I know nothing and which know nothing of me, I take fright and am amazed to see myself here rather than there: there is no reason for me to be here rather than there, now rather than then. Who put me here? by whose command and act were this time and place allotted to me?

Question 6. There are similarities between human beings and animals (e.g., both are material and die) but differences, too. The "spirit of man rises upward" and that of animals goes down to the earth (Ecclesiastes 3:21).

Question 11. A doctrine of God taken from Ecclesiastes 2–4 might include:

1. God gives happiness in normal life as a gift (2:24-25).
2. He judges evil eventually (3:17).
3. His actions are forever (3:14).
4. He can't be fully known or understood (3:11).
5. He has dealt us a hand that is a burden (3:10).
6. He performs a permanent, unchangeable action, but for a purpose (3:14).

It is characteristic of the literary form of the poetic books (Job through Ecclesiastes) that they overstate or exaggerate for effect their judgments. Solomon can be thought to speak at times in extremes. Your group may protest such pronouncements as not literally true; give them the freedom to argue with the text. Solomon is "thinking aloud" in these chapters and sometimes speaking with emotional abandon.

◼ Study 3/Making the Most of It

Question 1. Much of Ecclesiastes describes not what *ought* to be but *what is*. This is an important principle in interpreting Ecclesiastes, even though sometimes the reader cannot determine if the passage is simply describing a situation or commending it.

Question 8. In one sense, it's a lucky person who can just enjoy life and not brood over the human condition. Yet the negatives of life eventually catch up with us all. The counsel in Ecclesiastes 7:2 must be taken seriously ("the living should take this to heart"), meaning, if there are answers to life's problems, we should learn those answers as soon as possible.

◼ Study 4/Wisdom Is Worth the Trouble

Introductory comment: The concepts of *time* and *chance,* finally declared in Ecclesiastes 9:11, that figure into and permeate the mental wrestling of the Teacher reflect the limited viewpoint we have—ways the moth on the patterned rug would look at things. Many Christians are uncomfortable talking about chance since they believe God has the whole world in his hands. God is outside time and in control of events. But here is another way that Ecclesiastes needs to be carefully read. The world under the sun looks like it is vulnerable to chance, luck, or fate. Even for Christians it may look that way since they have the limitations of their own vision.

Question 2. In Ecclesiastes 12:9 the Teacher says he collected proverbs and sayings. Chapters 7–10 are largely proverbs and practical wisdom growing out of the Teacher's outlook on life.

Question 9. In light of this passage, discuss these words by Pope Paul VI, just before his death:

> Why have I not sufficiently studied, explored and admired the place in which life goes on? Such unpardonable distractions, such reprehensible superficialities. I would like finally to have a summing up and knowing notion of the world and life. I think that such a notion has to be expressed in grateful acknowledgment: Everything was a gift, everything was a grace. . . . [The] world is a bewitching panorama. It is lavishness without measure. . . . I am assailed with grief at not having admired this picture enough, at not having observed the worth of the wonders of nature.

■ Study 5/More Practical Wisdom Under the Sun

Question 1. The films of Woody Allen echo many themes of Ecclesiastes concerning the meaninglessness of life and the inevitability of death. Your group may have a taste for discussing an excerpt of one of his films such as *Love and Death* or *Hannah and Her Sisters* as a separate exercise or "case study."

Question 9. The Wisdom literature of Proverbs and Ecclesiastes gives us prudent courses of action that at least *improve* the odds of happiness and success, if not actually beat them.

Question 11. As you discuss this question, how does this quote relate? The Nazi architect Albert Speer, decades after the war ended, wrote this:

During the 20 years I spent in Spandau prison, I often asked myself what I would have done if I had recognized Hitler's real face and the true nature of the regime he had established. The answer was banal and dispiriting: My position as Hitler's architect had soon become indispensable to me. Not yet thirty, I saw before me the most exciting prospects an architect can dream of. Moreover, the intensity with which I went at my work repressed problems that I ought to have faced. A good many perplexities were smothered by the daily rush. In writing these memoirs I became increasingly astonished to realize that before 1944, I so rarely—in fact almost never—found the time to reflect about myself or my own activities, that I never gave my own existence a thought. (from *Inside the Third Reich*)

Question 12. The reality of a benevolent God is what keeps Ecclesiastes from pessimism, despair, and ultimately "vanity."

■ Study 6/The End of the Matter

Question 2. The themes of youth and old age will give a group opportunity to talk about the rewards and regrets of old age.

Question 5. Ecclesiastes assumes that God is the Creator and is sovereign behind the scenes.

3:11—God has the eternal view and has put that in our hearts.

5:19—God enables ordinary "gladness of heart" in everyday life.

7:29—He made us upright but we have fallen from that ideal.

11:5—He is the Maker and Sovereign over all events and has his own creative ways.

Question 8. Look for poor eyesight, deafness, lost teeth, mobility problems, energy deficit, decay, and more.

Question 9. Note the contrast between the pleasures of life in earlier parts of this book and the later years in which "you will say 'I find no pleasure in them'" (Ecclesiastes 12:1). Ecclesiastes doesn't deny the pleasures of life, nor does it sugarcoat the pains of life.

Question 10. The Teacher claims a link to Divine Wisdom rather than just clever insight of his own. The "Shepherd" is a further insight into the "Creator" of Ecclesiastes 12:1.

Question 12. Here, it may be helpful to discuss this modern conclusion by author Walker Percy:

> Life is much too much trouble, far too strange to arrive at the end of it and then to be asked what you make of it, and to have to answer: "scientific humanism." That won't do. A poor show. Life is a mystery, love is a delight. Therefore I take it as axiomatic that one should settle for nothing less than the infinite mystery and the infinite delight—that is, *God*. In fact, I demand it. I refuse to settle for anything else.

■ Study 7/Ecclesiastes and the Whole Bible

Question 2. Assign different passages to members of your group and invite them to recall where Ecclesiastes speaks with the same tone of voice. Some ideas might include:

Psalm 49:5-15—Mortality: The inevitable end of our lives, which relativizes and limits our earthly happiness.

1 Timothy 6:6-10—The folly of pursuing money, pleasure, ambition, which will never satisfy.

1 Timothy 6:17-19—At the same time, a healthy enjoyment of God's blessings in this life.

James 4:13-17—Time and chance, the apparent randomness of the events in every life, affects all our plans, yet God is the Ultimate Environment, the One finally "in charge."

1 Peter 3:8-17—The just person living in a world of injustice and unfairness in human relations.

Question 3. The Greek word for "vanity" or "frustration" in the New Testament is identical to the word for vanity in the Greek version of Ecclesiastes.

Question 7. The "Bible's night before Christmas" quote is from Robert Short in *A Time to Be Born—A Time to Die* (Harper, 1973). He suggests that Ecclesiastes is "essentially a kind of negative theologian, asking questions that can be answered only by a future revelation of God, and clearing the road for this revelation by smashing any and all false hopes to pieces." Do you agree?

In closing, how do these words by twentieth-century journalist, writer, and media personality, Malcolm Muggeridge reflect the message of Ecclesiastes?

I may, I suppose, regard myself or pass for being a relatively successful man. People occasionally stare at me in the streets—that's fame. I can fairly easily earn enough to qualify

for admission to the higher slopes of the Internal Revenue—
that's success. Furnished with money and a little fame even
the elderly, if they care to, may partake of trendy diversions—
that's pleasure. It might happen once in a while that something
I said or wrote was sufficiently heeded for me to persuade
myself that it represented a serious impact on our time—that's
fulfillment. Yet I say to you—and I beg you to believe me—
multiply these tiny triumphs by a million, add them all together, and they are nothing—less than nothing, a positive
impediment—measured against one draught of that living
water Christ offers to the spiritually thirsty, irrespective of
who or what they are. (Quoted in David Porter's *The Practical
Christianity of Malcolm Muggeridge,* InterVarsity Press,
1983.)

WHAT SHOULD WE STUDY NEXT?

To help your group answer that question, we've listed the Fisherman Guides by category so you can choose your next study.

TOPICAL STUDIES

Angels, Wright
Becoming Women of Purpose, Barton
Building Your House on the Lord, Brestin
The Creative Heart of God, Goring
Discipleship, Reapsome
Doing Justice, Showing Mercy, Wright
Encouraging Others, Johnson
The End Times, Rusten
Examining the Claims of Jesus, Brestin
Friendship, Brestin
The Fruit of the Spirit, Briscoe
Great Doctrines of the Bible, Board
Great Passages of the Bible, Plueddemann
Great Prayers of the Bible, Plueddemann
Growing Through Life's Challenges, Reapsome
Guidance & God's Will, Stark
Heart Renewal, Goring
Higher Ground, Brestin
Images of Redemption, Van Reken

Integrity, Engstrom & Larson
Lifestyle Priorities, White
Marriage, Stevens
Miracles, Castleman
One Body, One Spirit, Larsen
The Parables of Jesus, Hunt
Prayer, Jones
The Prophets, Wright
Proverbs & Parables, Brestin
Satisfying Work, Stevens & Schoberg
Senior Saints, Reapsome
Sermon on the Mount, Hunt
Spiritual Gifts, Dockrey
A Spiritual Legacy, Christensen
Spiritual Warfare, Moreau
The Ten Commandments, Briscoe
Ultimate Hope for Changing Times, Larsen
Who Is God? Seemuth
Who Is Jesus? Van Reken
Who Is the Holy Spirit? Knuckles & Van Reken
Wisdom for Today's Woman: Insights from Esther, Smith
Witnesses to All the World, Plueddemann
Women at Midlife, Miley
Worship, Sibley

BIBLE BOOK STUDIES

Genesis, Fromer & Keyes
Exodus, Larsen
Job, Klug
Psalms, Klug
Proverbs: Wisdom That Works,
Wright
Jeremiah, Reapsome
Jonah, Habakkuk, & Malachi,
Fromer & Keyes
Matthew, Sibley
Mark, Christensen
Luke, Keyes
John: Living Word, Kuniholm
Acts 1-12, Christensen
Paul (Acts 13-28), Christiansen
Romans: The Christian
Story, Reapsome
1 Corinthians, Hummel

Strengthened to Serve
(2 Corinthians),
Plueddemann
Galatians, Titus & Philemon,
Kuniholm
Ephesians, Baylis
Philippians, Klug
Colossians, Shaw
Letters to the Thessalonians,
Fromer & Keyes
Letters to Timothy, Fromer &
Keyes
Hebrews, Hunt
James, Christensen
1 & 2 Peter, Jude, Brestin
How Should a Christian Live?
(1, 2 & 3 John), Brestin
Revelation, Hunt

BIBLE CHARACTER STUDIES

David: Man after God's Own
Heart, Castleman
Elijah, Castleman
Great People of the Bible,
Plueddemann
King David: Trusting God for
a Lifetime, Castleman
Men Like Us, Heidebrecht &
Scheuermann

Moses, Asimakoupoulos
Paul (Acts 13-28), Christensen
Women Like Us, Barton
Women Who Achieved for
God, Christensen
Women Who Believed God,
Christensen

Printed in the United States
by Baker & Taylor Publisher Services